INTRODUCTION

This thematic package, based on **'Our Body'**, has been designed for lower primary students.

The activities have been organised into subject foci. Thematic programming ideas have been included so that teachers may integrate the theme across the curriculum.

A clip art page and answers have been included to save busy teachers valuable preparation time.

CONTENTS

Fully Reproducible Copymasters

Our Body

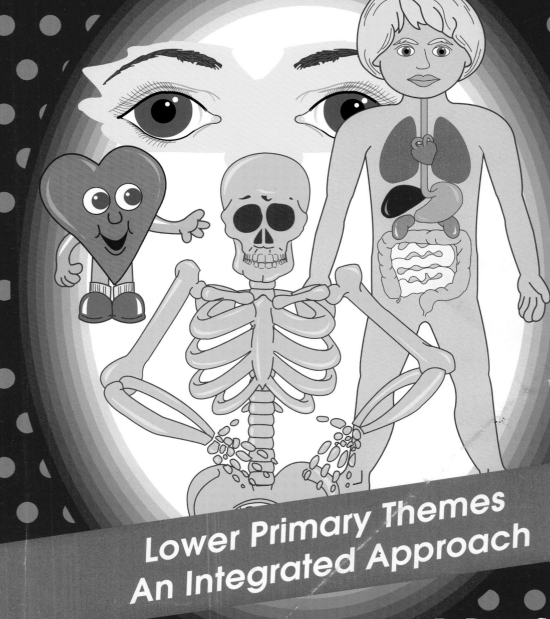

Lower Primary Themes
An Integrated Approach

By Donna Cocking

ISBN 1-86400-206-9

Prim-Ed
Publishing

9 781864 002065

Our Body
Prim-Ed Publishing

First published in 1993 by R.I.C. Publications
Reprinted in 1996 by R.I.C. Publications
Reprinted under license in 1996 and 1998 by Prim-Ed Publishing

Copyright Donna Cocking 1993

ISBN 1 86400 206 9
PR–0439

Additional titles available in this series:

All About Me	Christmas	Easter

Prim-Ed Publishing Pty. Ltd.
Offices in: United Kingdom: PO Box 051, Nuneaton, Warwickshire, CV11 6ZU
                  Australia: PO Box 332, Greenwood, Western Australia, 6024
                  Republic of Ireland: PO Box 8, New Ross, County Wexford, Ireland

£11.35

Our Body

ONE WEEK LOAN

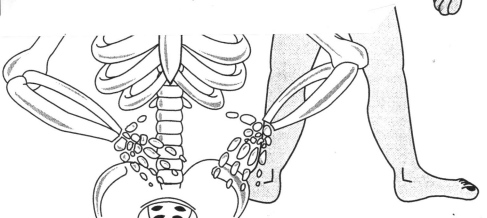

Written By

Donna Cocking

Prim-Ed Publishing

teaching practice.

THEME EXTENSION ACTIVITIES

Life cycle
Ageing
Life and death
Birth
Puberty

Impairment of the
five senses
Physical disabilities
Mental disabilities

Systems
Respiration
Circulation
Reproduction
Endocrine

Bones and joints
Movement
Coordination
Muscle tone

Physical/mental
Rest
Sleep
Exercise
Diet

People who help us
Hairdresser
Doctor, dentist
Physiotherapist
Dietitian

Songs
If you're happy . . .
Wriggle your toes
Punchinello
Dem Bones

Games
Orange chin pass
Lame dog
Hug tag

Art and Craft
Plasticine identikits
Stuffed dolls
Fancy dress
Mask Making

Visits
Museum
Hospital
Doctor's surgery
Retirement village

Poems
A Funny Man - N. Joan
When I Grow Up - W. Wise

Stories
Rosie's Walk - P. Hutchins
Anna's Silent World - B. Wolf

Clip Art for Busy Teachers

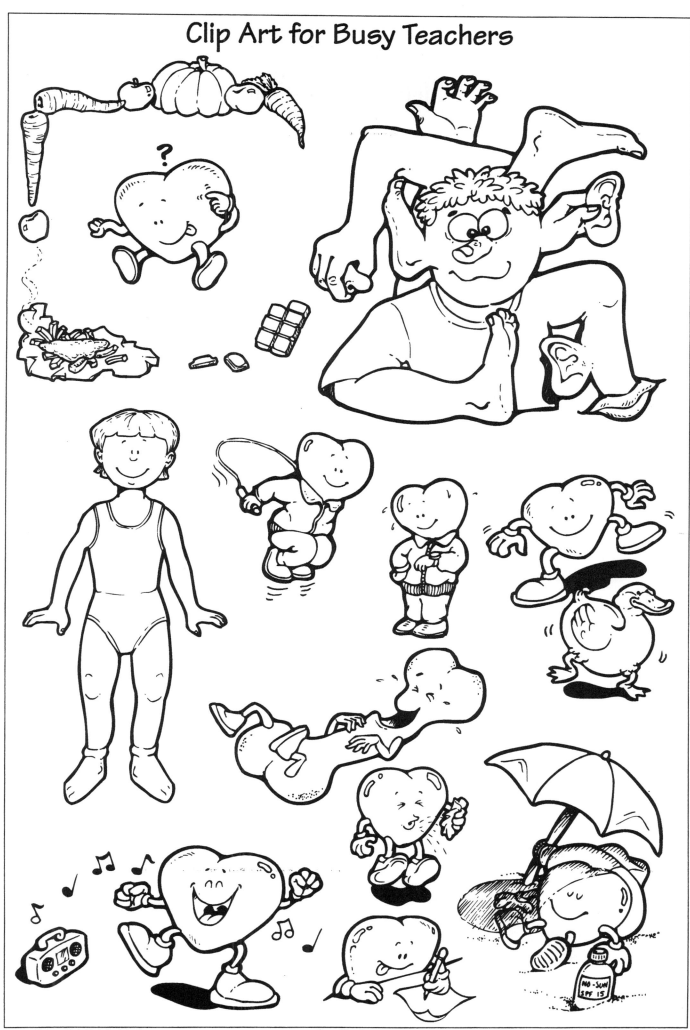

HEALTHY BODY - WORD SLEUTH

Find words from the sleuths below and put them under the correct heading.

M	E	A	T	D	O	R	T	H	O	D	O	N	T	I	S	T	C	B	C	O
I	A	T	O	O	T	H	P	A	S	T	E	I	R	O	F	S	H	G	E	W
L	B	E	E	L	O	A	D	V	T	O	R	N	U	R	S	E	K	N	R	B
K	R	B	I	E	P	J	S	U	R	G	E	O	N	E	U	W	O	D	E	E
T	F	R	U	V	T	Y	N	J	H	S	E	A	F	U	R	G	S	O	A	P
S	H	A	M	P	O	O	L	M	O	H	A	I	R	B	R	U	S	H	L	G
C	H	E	E	S	M	T	O	O	T	H	B	R	U	S	H	H	A	S	E	W
C	E	R	L	O	E	S	I	G	G	Y	P	O	I	P	J	F	A	O	S	L
B	R	E	A	D	T	A	P	E	V	E	G	E	T	A	B	L	E	G	T	E
D	O	C	T	O	R	E	D
S	C	E	G	S	I	L	E
E	H	J	F	T	S	R	N
N	E	B	R	E	T	P	T
S	E	G	G	S	A	E	I
C	S	D	E	O	T	G	S
I	E	U	F	R	Y	O	T

Healthy food.

meat _____   _____

_____   _____

_____   _____

_____   _____

People who care for our body.

_____   _____

_____   _____

_____   _____

Equipment we use to look after our body. _____

BODY WORDS

Write these words in alphabetical order.

face, ankle, brow, ear, chin   nose, teeth, neck, tongue, nail

1. _____   1. _____

2. _____   2. _____

3. _____   3. _____

4. _____   4. _____

5. _____   5. _____

Match these words to make compound words.

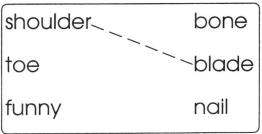

shoulder   bone
toe   blade
funny   nail

rib   lobe
ear   head
fore   cage

Make as many words as you can from the letters in the word...

- H E A R T B E A T -

_____

_____

_____

_____

NAME THE BODY PARTS

Write another name for these body parts.   Use these words.

ticker, cakehole, crown, pinkie, hooter, mop, peepers, scruff, pegs

eyes _____   heart _____   mouth _____

head _____   hair _____   neck _____

finger _____   nose _____   legs _____

Unjumble the body parts.

cekn

_____

mra

_____

dnha

_____

tofo _____   asctohm _____   gle _____

dhea

_____

ekne

_____

sthce

_____

npsei _____

Name the body part that rhymes with each word.

boulder _____   bed _____   peg _____

deer _____   key _____   bin _____

band _____   nest _____   zip _____

Write a word that rhymes with each body part.

tummy _____   eye _____   shin _____

mouth _____   toe _____   wrist _____

OUR BODY

Write these words and add 'ing'.

sleep _____   sing _____

run _____   swim _____

ride _____   smile _____

Use some of these 'ing' words to complete the sentences.

1. The children are _____ in the choir.

2. Our family enjoys _____ at the beach.

3. I like _____ my bike to school.

4. The baby is _____ in the pram.

5. The teacher is _____ for the photo.

6. The child is _____ across the park.

Use these words to complete the crosspatch.

ankle, arm, ear, elbow, eyebrow, head, heart,
lung, organ, shoulder, stomach, toe, wrist

MY MEASUREMENTS

Height _____

Hand span _____

Length of foot _____

Four classmates that are **taller/shorter** than me are:

	Name	Height
1		
2		
3		
4		

MY FACE

Hair colour _____

Eye colour _____

Complexion _____

Look at yourself carefully in the mirror and draw your face in the mirror below.

MY
BODY
BOOK

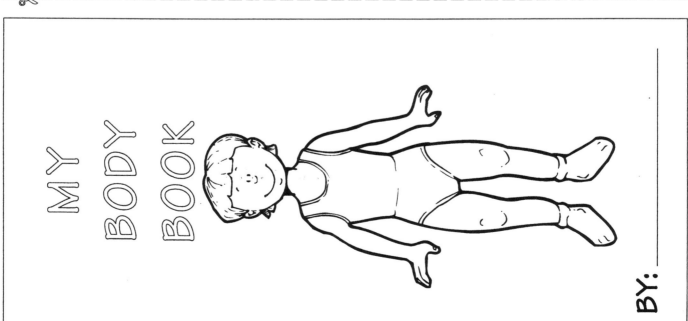

BY: _____

INTERESTING THINGS I CAN DO

☐ I can whistle.

☐ I can wink.

☐ I can touch my toes.

☐ I can click my fingers.

☐ I can touch my nose with my tongue.

☐ I can wiggle my ears.

☐ I can wiggle my eyebrows.

☐ I can _____

MY TEETH

There are three main types of _____. The front teeth (_____) are flat, broad and used for biting. The side teeth (_____) are sharp, pointed and used for tearing. The back teeth (_____) are large, double teeth, used for grinding and chewing.

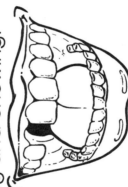

I have lost _____ teeth.

I have _____ incisors.

I have _____ canines.

I have _____ molars.

TIMING MYSELF

A pulse is the regular beating caused by the contractions of the heart. Find a pulse on your body and measure it for 60 seconds.

My pulse rate is _____ beats per minute.

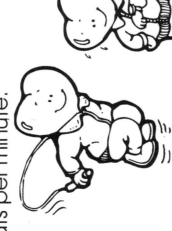

In 30 seconds I can...

bounce a ball _____ times.

write my name _____ times.

skip with a rope _____ times.

PRODUCT LABELS

Use some of these words and phrases to label the products below.

protects hands, no more tangles, soft and gentle, water
resistant, gentle on eyes, one pair, maximum protection,
premium quality, household, nourishing, family pack, SPF 15+,
flock-lined, normal to oily, 2-ply, broad spectrum

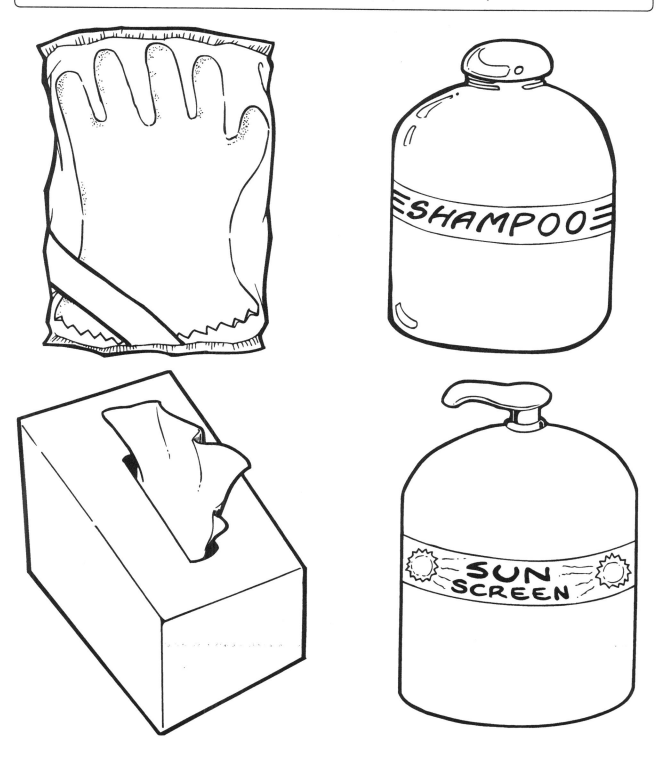

Design your own toothpaste label.

QUICK QUIZ

Use these words to answer the quiz questions.

> ankle, blood, bones, ear, eye, eyelid, fingers, heart, iris, knee, legs, neck, nose, ribs, shoulder, skin, teeth, tongue

1. The protective layer which covers our body. _____

2. Limbs used for running and jumping. _____

3. Joins the arm to the neck and body. _____

4. Organ used for smelling. _____

5. Coloured part of the eye. _____

6. Organ used for seeing. _____

7. A covering which protects the eye. _____

8. Organ used for hearing. _____

9. Connects the head to the rest of the body. _____

10. Organ used for taste. _____

11. A cage of bone which protects the lungs. _____

12. Used for biting and chewing food. _____

13. Parts found at the end of the hand. _____

14. Organ which pumps blood through the body. _____

15. Part which connects the leg to the foot. _____

16. Area between the lower and upper leg. _____

17. Fluid that carries oxygen around the body. _____

18. Hard tissue which makes up the skeleton. _____

DOT - TO - DOT

Join the dots then label these body parts. Use pencil to make sure you have joined the correct dots.

ankle, arm, chest, chin, ear, finger, foot, hand, head, knee, leg, neck, nose, shoulder, stomach, thigh, toe, navel

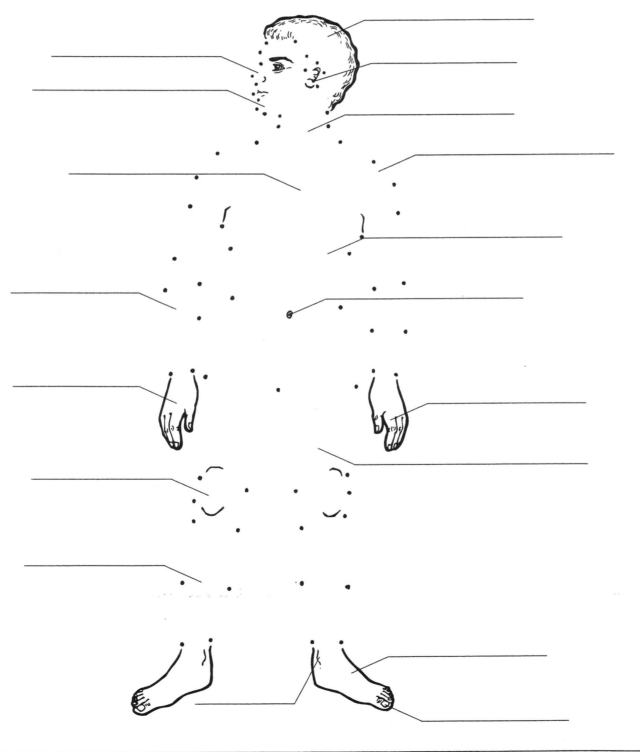

SKELETON MATHS

- Write the sums that equal **15** on the **skull**.

- Write the sums that equal **18** on the **rib bones**.

- Write the sums that equal **20** on the **arm bones**.

- Write the sums that are left over around the **outside** of the skeleton.

16 - 1 =	10 x 2 =	9 x 2 =	5 x 5 =
13 + 2 =	3 x 5 =	3 x 6 =	6 + 7 =
25 - 5 =	10 + 8 =	9 + 6 =	20 - 2 =
14 + 4 =	18 - 5 =	15 + 5 =	11 + 7 =
5 x 4 =	12 + 8 =	9 + 3 =	10 +10 =

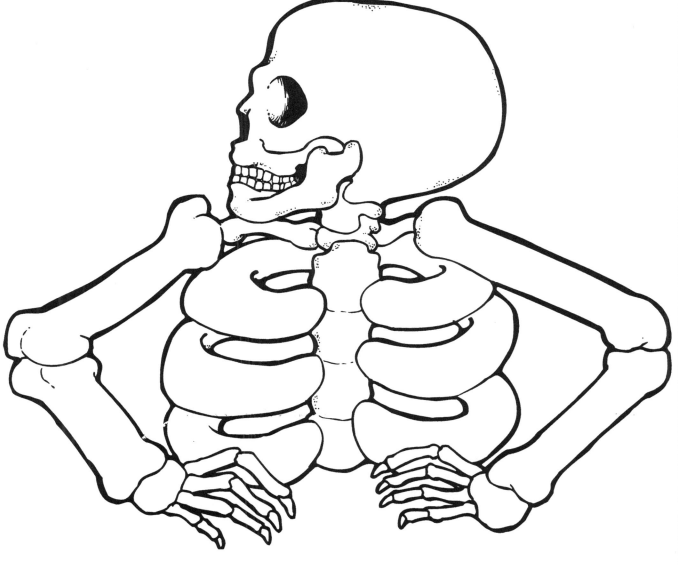

BRAINS AND MEMORY

Study these numbers for 30 seconds, then cover them.

1   7   6   9   3   2   4   8

Write them in the order they occurred.

_____

Study these numbers for 30 seconds, then cover them.

2   4   6   8   10   12   14   16   18   20

Write them in the order they occurred.

_____

Which set of numbers was easier to remember?   Why?

_____

_____

Study this list of objects for 30 seconds, then cover them.

 tea-towel, ladder, desk, pot, tile, banana, glass, flower

Write down the things that you remember from the list.

_____

_____

Study this list of objects for 30 seconds, then cover them.

pencil, pen, crayon, felt pen, glue, ruler, eraser, sharpener

Write down the things that you remember from the list.

_____

_____

Discuss which set of objects was easier to remember?   Why?

CLASS DATA

How many students have:

brown eyes _____

green eyes _____

blue eyes _____

hazel eyes _____

Measure, record and graph the heights of students in the class.

Who is the tallest?

_____

Who is the shortest?

_____

How many students:

walk to school? _____

ride a bicycle to school? _____

are driven to school in a car? _____

travel to school in a bus? _____

How many students dislike:

broccoli _____

peas _____

chocolate _____

apples _____

fish and chips _____

Who has the longest hair? _____

Who has the shortest hair? _____

How many students have:

dark hair? _____

fair hair? _____

curly hair? _____

straight hair? _____

THE EYE - 1

Use these words to label the parts of the eye.

pupil, iris, eyelashes, eyelid, eyeball, tear duct, eyebrow

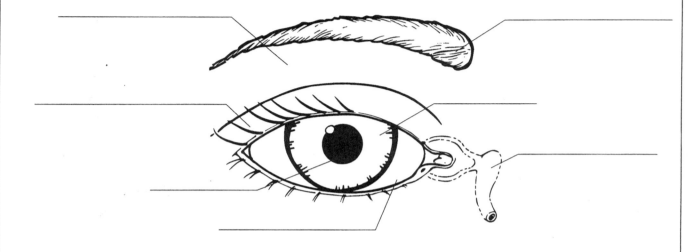

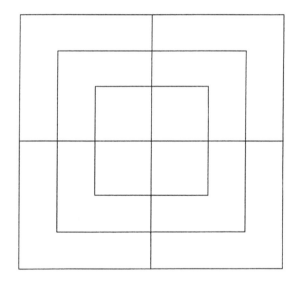

How many squares make up this eye puzzler?

_____

Make up your own eye puzzler using circles, triangles or rectangles.

Can you read this eye chart when you are standing three metres away?

F

E G P

K W V Y D S N

R M X C T

B J O Z L

A U I Q

THE EYE - 2

The eye is the camera for the brain. As light rays enter the eye, the information is passed through the pupil and onto the retina, which is like a projection screen. Nerves carry the screen message to the brain and the brain decodes what has been seen. The eye is a sensitive, delicate body organ. The eyelashes, eyebrows and eyelids protect the eye from dust particles and harsh light.

Look closely at a friend's eye and draw what you see.

Look at the size of the pupil.

• What happens to the size of the pupil when torch light is shone into the eye?

_____

_____

_____

• What will happen to the pupil when the eye is in complete darkness?

_____

_____

_____

• How should you take special care of your eyes?

_____

_____

_____

_____

_____

• Look carefully at the colours of the iris and describe its appearance.

_____

_____

_____

_____

_____

• Find out why some people need to wear glasses.

THE NOSE

Use these words to label the parts of the nose.

tip

bridge

nostril

septum

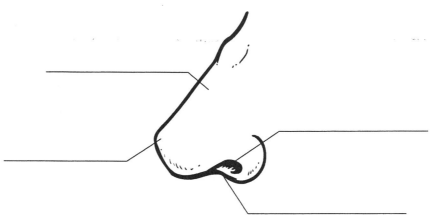

Here are some strange noses.
Can you guess the animal behind each one?

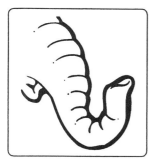   

_____ _____

The nose contains the nostrils, which provide a path for air during breathing. The nose is also the smelling organ.

Here are some things that smell.

Name and draw four other things that smell.

_____ _____ _____ _____

THE EAR

The outer ear is large and cup-shaped to collect waves of sound. The waves are guided through to the eardrum. They vibrate against the drum and are amplified by three bones:-
    the hammer;
    the stirrup; and
    the anvil.
Sounds then pass into the inner ear where they are caught by the shell-like cochlea. The sounds travel through the cochlea on a roller coaster ride to the brain. The brain then translates the sound into meaning.

Use these words to label the parts of the ear.

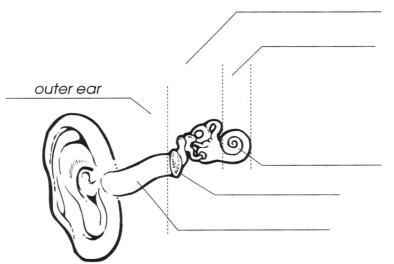

outer ear

outer ear
inner ear
canal
eardrum
middle ear
cochlea

Close your eyes.
Your teacher will make or play five sounds.
Can you guess what they are?

Guess		**Sound**	
1.	_____	1.	_____
2.	_____	2.	_____
3.	_____	3.	_____
4.	_____	4.	_____
5.	_____	5.	_____

THE MOUTH

The mouth is a special body organ which has parts responsible for the sounds of speech, chewing, eating and tasting food and the production of saliva.

Use these words to label the parts of the mouth.

upper lip

lower lip

teeth

tongue

gums

palate

uvula

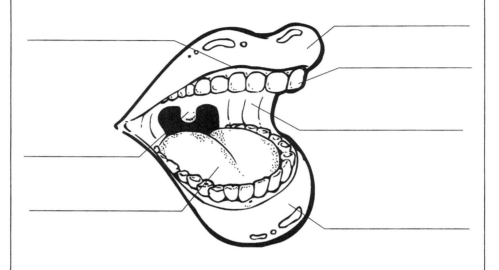

Add 'ing' to these words and write the mouth part responsible for each action.

Word	Action	Mouth Part
lick	licking	tongue
bite		
taste		
kiss		
chew		

Write four things you can taste and show whether you like or dislike them.

Food	Like	Dislike

TEETH

Teeth are used mainly for chewing our food, so that it is ready for digestion. The teeth are very hard, almost like bone. They are found in the mouth, growing out of the top and bottom jaws. The teeth chop and grind our food into smaller pieces. As the food moves around the mouth, it is mixed with saliva which makes the food soft and easy to swallow. The tongue helps to move the food around in our mouth.

Our teeth also help us to talk. The teeth and the tongue are used to make the different sounds needed to make up the words we speak.

Use these words to label the parts of the tooth.

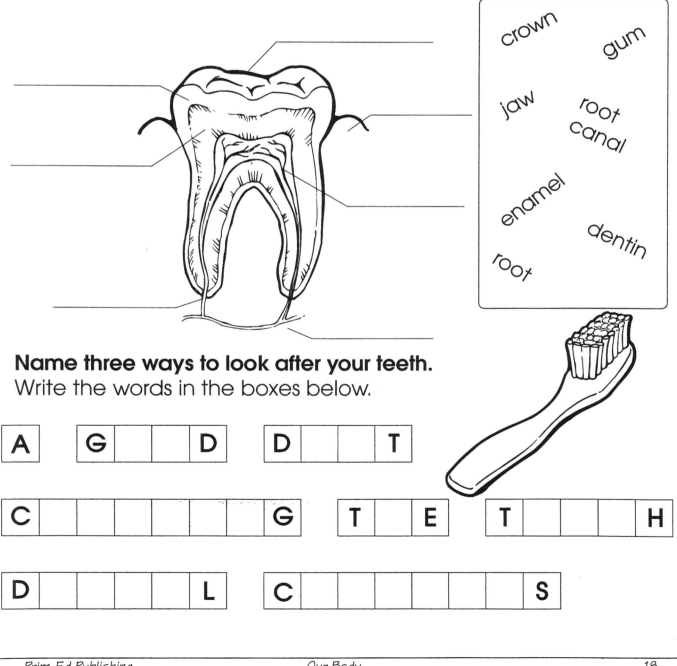

crown   gum

jaw   root canal

enamel   dentin

root

Name three ways to look after your teeth.
Write the words in the boxes below.

A	G			D	D			T

C					G	T	E	T			H

D				L	C					S

OPERATION GAME - 1

RULES:
Players take turns to throw the die, but can not begin playing until the number one has been thrown. When number one is thrown, that player glues the heart on the patient's body. Players continue to throw the die, following the order of the operation. The winner is the player who first completes the operation in order.

YOU WILL NEED:

- a die
- glue
- the patient
- scissors
- six body pieces

Cut out the six body pieces below. They must be glued in the following order, when the die is thrown.

1. heart

2. stomach

3. kidneys

4. lungs

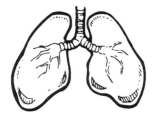

5. leg bone

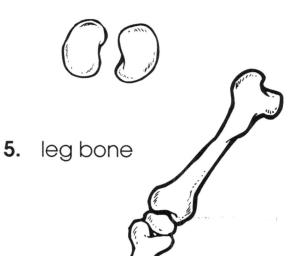

6. brain

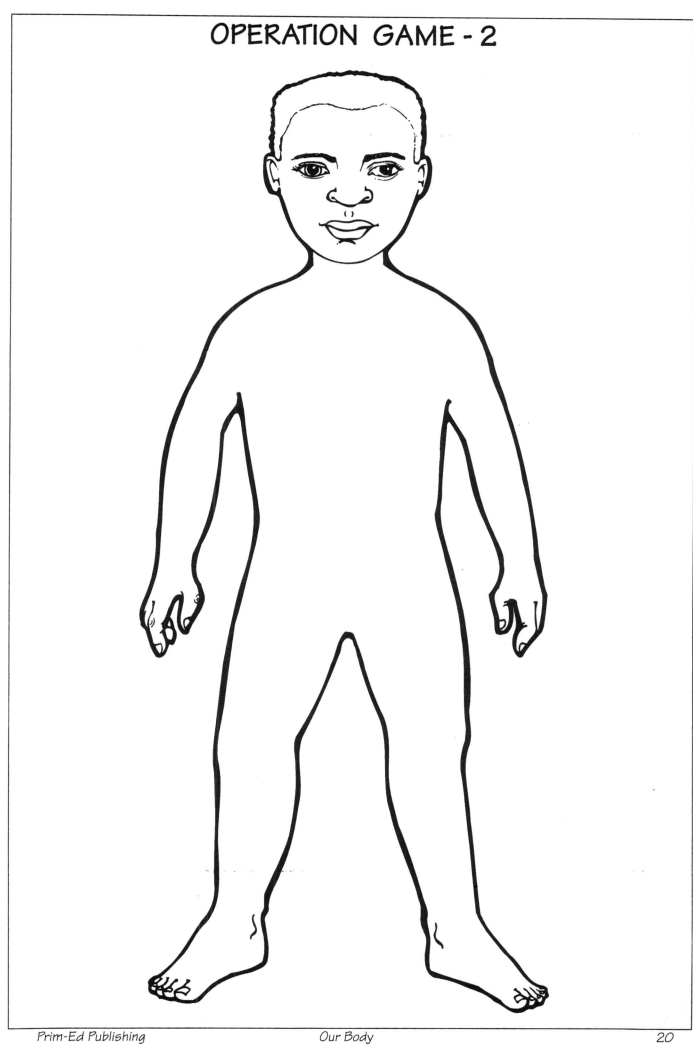

FIRST AID

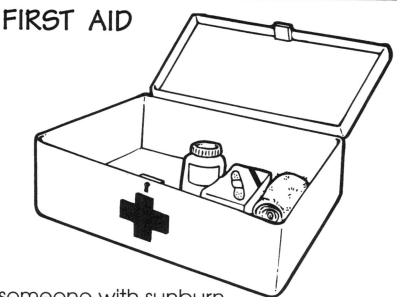

Draw and label another three important items to have in a first aid kit.

It is important to have a first aid kit for minor accidents, such as cuts, bruises, burns, bites and stings.

We could give first aid to someone with sunburn.

Cause:
Sunburn is caused by too much exposure to the harmful rays of the sun.

Prevention:
1. Regularly apply protective cream.
2. Wear a sunhat and protective clothing.
3. Avoid long periods in the sun.

Treatment:
1. Have a cool shower or bath.
2. Apply antiseptic cream or calamine lotion.

How would you give first aid to someone with a small cut?

Cause:
A small cut can be _____

_____

Prevention:

1. _____

2. _____

Treatment:

1. _____

2. _____

VISITING THE DOCTOR

Write about a time you visited the doctor.

Start out by telling why you needed to visit the doctor.

_____

_____

_____

_____

Describe your visit to your doctor.

Setting	Events
_____	_____
_____	_____
_____	_____
_____	_____
_____	_____

Finish by telling us how you came to feel well again.

Finish

_____

_____

_____

_____

_____

TREATMENT OF ILLNESS

The table below has information about the common cold and chickenpox.

Complaint	Symptoms	Treatment
Common Cold	Sneezing, runny nose, watery eyes, dry, sore throat, a cough and a temperature are all symptoms of the common cold.	Bed rest may be necessary. Drink plenty of fluids. Keep warm. Treat with medicine for pain and fever. Visit a doctor if symptoms continue for more than seven days.
Chickenpox	Highly infectious for 14 - 21 days. May begin with a high temperature and discomfort as red or pink spots first appear on the back, stomach and chest. These spots change to watery blisters and crust over.	Young children can wear gloves or cut their nails as scratching can cause infection. Bathe in a cool bath. Treat with a medicated soap or antiseptic solution. Rest is important.

Choose one of these and complete the table below.

splinter, bee sting, measles, ant bite, snake bite

Complaint	Symptoms	Treatment

Choose one other to complete on the back of this page.

BICYCLE SAFETY

It is very important to be a safe road user. When we ride our bicycle, we must always be careful and safe.

If you were to ride your bicycle to school and home again, what would you need to wear?

1. | H | | | | | |

2. | S | | | | |

3. | B | | | | | |

| C | | | | | | | |

Safety Quiz

1. Is it safe to ride in the middle of the road?   YES / NO

2. Should you have an adult with you?   YES / NO

3. Is it safe to ride at night?   YES / NO

4. Should you ride on the pavement?   YES / NO

5. Is it safe to ride through a group of people?   YES / NO

6. Should you walk your bike across the road?   YES / NO

Design a bright outfit that you could wear while riding your bicycle.

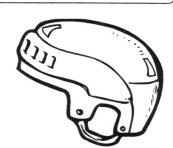

KEEPING PHYSICALLY FIT

To feel healthy, you must be fit. Feeling fit, gives you energy and strength to fight off illness.

Make sure you warm your whole body before doing any exercise. Here are some ideas:

- Lightly jog on the spot;
- March around using your arms and strong leg movements; or Dance to your favourite song.

When your body is warm, try the following activities. You will need:

- a stopwatch or clock
- a partner
- fifty metres of outdoor space
- markers

How long does it take you to:

walk 50 metres, backwards? _____

crab-walk 50 metres? _____

duck-waddle 50 metres? _____

skip 50 metres? _____

List two ways in which you could improve your recorded times.

1. Practise each activity regularly.

2. _____

3. _____

Explain why you think it is important to keep physically fit.

_____

_____

_____

CLAP YOUR HANDS

Use different body parts to complete the verse to this song.

Head, shoulders, knees and toes

Knees and toes

Head, shoulders, knees and toes

Knees and toes

Eyes, ears, mouth and nose

Head , shoulders, knees and toes

Knees and toes

Lips, hips, feet and thighs

Feet and thighs

_____

_____

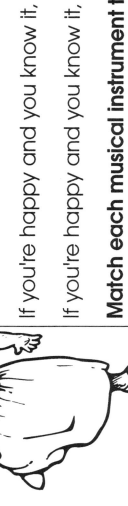

Write other lines to the song *If you're happy and you know it* then perform your actions.

If you're happy and you know it, clap your hands.

If you're happy and you know it, _____

If you're happy and you know it, _____

If you're happy and you know it, _____

If you're happy and you know it, _____

If you're happy and you know it, _____

If you're happy and you know it, _____

Match each musical instrument to the body action.

bang   guitar

blow   triangle

strum   trumpet

shake   tambourine

strike   maracas

WOOLLEN DOLL

You will need:

- thick wool
- scissors
- a book (15 cm long)
- scrap material
- felt pieces
- a book (30 cm long)

Instructions for arms:

- Wind wool around the length of the book 15 cm long, until about 3 cm wide.
- Slide from the book, tie each end in a knot, then cut.

Instructions for hair and head:

- Wind wool around the length of the book 30 cm long, until about 6 cm wide.
- Slide from the book, tie one end in a knot, then cut for hair.
- Leave a 3-cm gap, then tie again, for head.

Instructions for body, legs and feet:

- Split the remaining wool and slide through the arms.
- Leave a 5-cm gap, for body, then tie in a knot.
- Divide the remaining wool in half for each leg.
- Tie a knot at the end of each leg, for feet, then cut.

Decorate:

- Cut felt pieces for eyes, mouth and nose.
- Make clothes from scrap material.

PLASTER CASTING

You will need:

- plasticine
- ice-cream containers
- paints and brushes
- scrap materials

- mixing plaster
- a bowl
- scissors
- sandpaper

Instructions:

- Roll plasticine flat and thick, then place in the ice-cream container.

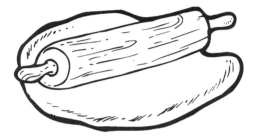

- Mix the plaster according to the directions.

- When plaster is set, cut away ice-cream container.

- Use sandpaper to remove any rough pieces of unwanted plaster.

- Use different body parts to cast shapes. For example, finger, hand, foot, toe, knee, elbow or tooth.

- Pour over mould and leave to set.

- Peel away the plasticine.

- Decorate by painting or adding scrap materials to the moulds. For example, a ring and nail polish could liven up a hand.

Answers

Page 1:

Healthy food - milk, eggs, cereal, vegetable, meat, cheese, fruit, bread.

People who care for our body - doctor, dentist, surgeon, orthodontist, optometrist, nurse.

Equipment we use to look after our body - toothbrush, shampoo, toothpaste, hairbrush, soap.

Page 3:

Write another name for these body parts - eyes = peepers, heart = ticker, mouth = cakehole, head = crown, hair = mop, neck = scruff, nose = hooter, legs = pegs

Unjumble the body parts - neck, head, arm, knee, hand, chest, foot, stomach, leg, spine.

Page 8:

Quick quiz -

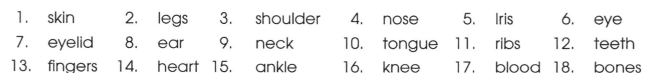

1. skin	2. legs	3. shoulder	4. nose	5. Iris	6. eye
7. eyelid	8. ear	9. neck	10. tongue	11. ribs	12. teeth
13. fingers	14. heart	15. ankle	16. knee	17. blood	18. bones

Page 13:

Eye puzzler - 15 squares.

Page 18:

Name three ways to look after your teeth -

1. A good diet   2. Cleaning the teeth.   3. Dental checkups.

Page 23:

Safety on a bicycle - 1. Helmet   2. Shoes   3. Bright clothes

Safety quiz - 1. No   2. Yes   3. No   4. No   5. No   6. Yes